TRUTH IN RHYME

Renée McRae

Jean,

Know what you want and never accept less!

Renée

DEDICATED IN LOVE

To my two daughters, Sumayah Hadiya and June Pearl

THANK YOU FOR YOUR PATIENCE AND SUPPORT

Mom, Jeff and Aunt Ethel

ACKNOWLEDGEMENT

My spiritual guide, Anand,
Without whom this could not be.

*"You Cannot Become Empowered
Until You Know The Truth"*

Renée McRae

Front Cover Design by Daryl Landy
Back Photograph by Judi Raines

TRUTH IN RHYME

INTRODUCTION

I begin by saying that I am honored to have been asked by my dear friend Radha (you may know her by the name Renée) to write a preface to her first book of poems. My initial thought was that this would be "a piece of cake", one of the easier things I'd been asked to do in life. After all, I have admired Radha's work from the first time I heard it. Yet, when it came time to write I had difficulty finding the words. What can be said of one so gifted, so special to me; and what light could I possibly shed on her poems -- each one so impassioned and complete. So I'm writing about the one thing I feel qualified to speak on in terms of Radha and that is the uniqueness of our friendship.

Upon our meeting, some ten years ago, at a Tai Chi demonstration in New Jersey, there was an instantaneous recognition of the Seeker's lineage to which we both belong. That night marked the reuniting of kindred souls for the purpose of growth and experience on a new plane of reality. And it was as if everyone present that night sensed, in some way, the significance of this meeting; it was magical. I will never forget Radha and I surrounded by ecstatic friends as we gazed at the starlit sky reciting each other's poems. Those were high times in the Universe because that experience spoke of the kind of friendship that continues to evolve. To this day the genuine bond of unconditional love and understanding that we share serves as a base for all our creative endeavors.

That I am in any way part of this creation of Radha's, this symbolic gift of her depth and understanding, is truly gratifying to me. It is about creation ... the mission ... the work to be done.

Marcia Parks

A NOTE FROM THE AUTHOR

For the past ten years I have drunk beer and belched. What I mean by that is that in various given situations, I drank the beer of life and upon the digestion of the experience, I belched out a poem describing my perception of that experience. As I have stated in most of my recitations, I consider all of my experiences as unwritten poems; and I like to think of all of my poems as *Truth in Rhyme.*

Inasmuch as I have accepted that language is a couple of steps away from Truth -- actions even being a step away -- I have attempted in the writing of this book to convey through the language commonly termed "poetry" (what I consider to be at least three steps away) my thoughts, feelings, emotions, frustrations, fears and desires.

Usually a person will relate to the poetry through their own prior experiences. Occasionally, however, I am asked my feelings about a particular piece and what my personal experience was that inspired that poem. To that end I have given a brief commentary on some of the poetry you will read in the pages that follow.

It is my hope that you enjoy this compilation.

TABLE OF CONTENTS

I AM

I AM

Not the Mind.

As does the baby exist without language, definitions, mind chatter, morals, judgments, etc., so do I exist separate and apart from the mind. What need I of labels?

1

All I Know is what I Feel
All Else is of the Mind
In Dropping the Mind
We Come to the Real
All Else is Left Behind.

The bottom line of living is feeling. The Truth in life is the feeling in the moment, not what I think about the feeling or the label I place upon the feeling, but the actual feeling I get from the energy in the moment.

Sometimes It's Hard To Be

Happy About Just Being

Sometimes it's hard to be happy

About just being alive

Without you

and then

I remember.

Was it Shakespeare who said "To be or not to be, that is the question"? In my method of living (philosophy of life), the most important key to the secret of life is *to be*. To live in each moment fully and completely; so much so that there can be nothing else in that moment. There is no consideration of, guilt about, frustration over or any thing or thought that would take me away from the feeling of the energy of the moment.

WHY DO I THINK OF YOU?

Why do I think of you so much?
Maybe it's because of your touch.
But then again -
Maybe it's because of your grin.

I'd like to think it's neither
But then, I should not think
So from now on into the future
I will think of you /not/
for any reason,
And love you for — no thing.

This poem is a reflection of an attempt at what is commonly termed "unconditional love." For instance, a touch indicates a physical attraction, and a grin indicates a soulful attraction. But either one is a reason or a condition. To love for no reason is to be in a State of Grace or to be in a Oneness with the Universe allowing love to just emanate.

THIS LOVE FOR YOU

This love for you has truly outshone
Anything I have known
But I must let it go
This I know
If only but to live my own life

You see, magic and mindreading
and astral projection
All of these are traps
And when my love for you
Gets me all confused
It, too, holds me back

It can become an obsession
And in walks possession
You know this will not do
It's such a fine line
We have to walk
Enjoying but not indulging

We've come so far
Yet gone nowhere
We have a good many doors to open
We have to take it in stride
Let it be our guide
And never lose our direction.

Pointing to the trappings in our society that truly hold us back, this work reminds us to continue to stay focused on accomplishment. Magic and mindreading and astral projection are what I call branches on a tree of our evolution; the roots being the foundation and the trunk of the tree being the correct path. I used this analogy but it could in fact be anything that *dis-tracts* (takes you off the track) from the main goal or purpose in your life. In my opinion love has been one of the main distractions far too long. Not that I am against love, don't get me wrong. It is the way we have become accustomed to loving, the way we have been taught to love, programmed to love. Women, for instance have been taught to look for the fairytale ending — and we look — behind every pillar, post, up under every rock, talk about leaving no stone unturned! We have become *obsessed* with the idea of love and marriage. It is unfortunate we have not on a whole been taught to have other directions in our lives that we place equal or more importance upon.

You think that I may want your man
This may or may not be
You see, something deep inside me
Pulls him close, still closer to me

Our relations should not be upset
Since it's really not between us
We are but representations of
What's really deep within us

Although I know it seems
That we are pulling in join
But the struggle is in pulling on
Opposite sides of the same coin.

What you hold so dear and close to you
Is not what I want for me
What I see is a continuation
Of another reality

My mind would like to see your plight
And talk and even cater
But what it cannot understand
'Tis but a calculator.

I guess what I am trying to say,
Is, as Renée - this man is not my choice.
If you wish the deal
This thing is all unreal

It doesn't even exist.

This piece indicates that there is something going on between this man and woman that is not readily visible (reflected in the the first line). There is something happening between them separate and aside from what is termed 'physical reality', yet it is still being looked at and judged as a normal male-female sexual attraction. This is reflected in the line "Although I know it seems that we are pulling in join . . ." Sometimes there can be non-intentional psychic and telepathic communication, and if we are not used to experiencing this type of communication, it can lead one to believe that it must be an "act of God" or "I know this is meant to be, I wasn't even thinking about being with this person".

The mistake is in attempting to do something about the bond that is now shared. Love can be clean, open and nothing has to be done about it. It doesn't have to be anything more than what it is. Unfortunately, the habit is to now think it has to mean something: We've got to live together, be together, commit to own each other, deny any feelings we may have toward anyone who is or could be in our lives in whatever capacity -- for the sake of the other.

IF YOU CAN IMAGINE

If you can imagine a bird in flight
Loving the space he flies in
And you can imagine a fish in water
Loving the space he swims in

Then you can imagine a girl in New York
Whose only problem is being distraught
For she finally found the love of her life
But then, she wanted to be his wife.

Like a fish needs water
Like a bird seeks flight
The longing and yearning
Disturbed the night.

Frustrating it is when the knowledge
of truth
Interrupts the indulgence
in fiction
Preventing the liberty of feeling emotions
without guilt.

"Stay Close Inside"
Stay close inside?
How can this not be?

"Stay Close Inside"
Stay close inside?
You are a part of me.

"Stay Close Inside"
Stay close inside?
How can I otherwise do?

"Stay Close Inside"
Stay close inside?
I am a part of you.

THANK YOU FOR YOUR LOVE

Thank you for your love
Thank you for your caring
And thank you most of all
For sincerity in sharing

Thank you so much
For not taking advantage
Of a love that was
Offered on a platter

Through your unselfishness you
Have helped and guided me
Through a passageway I may
Have otherwise taken years
To get through - or even find

By your very thoughts
You have influenced my actions
By your actions
You have influenced my very thoughts

I will love you always
And thank you eternally

Love here has no greater desire
Than to be returned
Thank you for letting me
See love somewhere else

Although this seems like goodbye
We know that can never be
Spread your love and I'll spread mine
Maybe one glorious day
We'll get back around to each other.

I GO TO WORK

I go to work every day
Just to make that money
Trying to ignore the madness in me,
Acting sweet as honey

I'm a madman I know
But I can't let it show
Because no one would believe

How excited I get
In an internal sweat
And Lord, don't you know

It's times like these
If I could only but sneeze
Or anything to take away

This awful pain inside
Under my calm outside
That seems to go on for weeks

And the craziest part -
It may give you a start -
I think I'm in the wrong body!

I've got to get across to you
The power of your voice
It touches something deep in me
And takes away my choice

To feel anything but good inside
And in that I rejoice

Your velvet covered vocal chords
Encapsulate my soul
Surrounding me with all that's good
And blocks me from the cold

Your softness and your quiet strength
Inherent in your tone
Caresses me in gentleness
That comes right through the phone.

I Miss You 🦋

Your touch, your smile, your eyes, your laugh

Your laugh is joyous, genuine, real

Your touch is so full of energy - - - so vibrant

Your eyes are intense, so open, so you

Your smile is loving, caring, sensitive

You are such an illuminated being

I could dive into you and be in ecstacy.

Tomorrow we'll try harder
Tomorrow we'll go farther
Funny - how tomorrow never comes.

Tomorrow we will give our all
Tomorrow we will never fall
Funny - how tomorrow never comes.

Tomorrow is forever
Tomorrow is never
Tomorrow is a sickness
We use it to escape from today.

Thank you for setting me free
For giving me the chance to be me

To explore and unfold
The many stories untold
In my present and past
Which goes, so fast

Hoping and skipping
Through life we go
Not even thinking
Of what we don't know

Not giving a care
To what we could share
If we only but knew
What really lies there

Tomorrow is new
And all because you
Took the time to show me
This world is not true

No words can describe
The feelings inside
The memories we hold
Of when we were bold

There is no forgetting
But there is acceptance.

These words I dedicate to my spiritual guide, Anand.

GIVE ME A BREAK! 🦋

What is this thing
We call it Life
Hustle, bustle
Struggle and strife

Where do we come from
And where does it end
I mean, are we in control
Or at the mercy of the wind

Where are we going
Is anybody sure
I mean, what the heck is this
Is there a cure

Give me a break!
Is often our plea
We're becoming like doctors
In failing to see

That we're treating the symptoms
And not the cause
Dig deep inside, my friend
You'll find yours.

Find what it is
That makes YOU tick
Sooner or later
Something will click

(Cont'd.)

Some day - some way
Some time in space
You will find
Your Original Face

Live your life
It was given to you
There is so much to gain
On this plane

Grab all you can
While passing through
And use it all
Enjoying the new.

One afternoon while driving home from a friend's, I began to question existence - mine for one. I am sorry to say, I was depressed - in a funk. I wondered why I was on this planet, anyway. I couldn't have been born for nothing. Did I have a purpose? What was it? I wondered where are we anyway? The all-too-familiar words came back. We're on Earth. What is *Earth?* We're in America ... New York ... Hollis ... daytime ... nighttime ... Winter ... Spring ... inside ... outside ... in the car, etc. Nothing would satisfy me. Who made up those words, anyway? I mean, they're just *words*. I began to realize we have become so comfortable with a language we've been taught to describe where we are, that we don't even *question* where we are anymore. We know already. And so, in desperation, I beseeched the Universe with the above poem.

By Whose Standards

When you look at me
Through your mind's eye
Do you see me?
Or do you see
What you think you see?
Which is not really seeing, at all.

I do not wear my hair as you would like
Nor do I clothe myself in fashions
of your choice
Does that make me less?
By whose standards?

I like it short and curly
I like it long and straight
I like it above my knees
I like it to the floor
And most times in between

I choose my looks
According to my moods

I cannot judge
My brain is but a computer
It will cease to function
If I am not in it.

*If by some freak of nature
My skin changed color
Would I still be me?*

Would you still love me?

Would I still love me?

*Should I be glad I'm not
Or sorry I am
Your child?*

WHY IS IT WE ARE BLIND

Why is it we are blind
Why can't we see the trap
Why can we not awaken
Like the early morning birds?

Why can't we see the future
Instead of just the past
How can we not know
If we had this dream before?

Why is it if we know,
We cannot recognize
The dreams are interwoven
Forming illusions of confusion

When will the mind
Set the spirit free from bondage
When will we be able
To out-step this mighty web?

Don't let Life
Get you Down
Get right off
That Merry-go-Round

Jump back
Stand back
Look at it Straight
See if you
Can Determine Your Fate

Try if you will
Say a little Prayer
God, please take me
Out of Despair

Show me the Way
Whatever the Cost
Show me the Way
For I am Lost.

WHEN I THINK OF YOU I AM SADDENED

When I think of you I am saddened
Because what we had - we no longer have

I know I must go on living
A defeatist I've never been
Yet, sometimes I can't help the urge
To stop at a familiar tree, or corner or place
That could very well be my bedroom
Lying on my bed staring into space
And seeing something familiar
Focusing in - and realizing it's a
Recently framed picture of you and I
At a very happy time

And when I think of you I am saddened
Because what we had - we no longer have

All grins we were, I remember that trip
Standing on the railing of a cruise ship
Going no where in particular
But enjoying each other all the way there
Drinks in our hands, love in our eyes
Me leaning on you, you leaning on me
A perfect picture of love and happiness
I am saddened when I think of you
Because what we had - we no longer have

A shift of the eyes - and all is null
For what we are Here for
Has nothing to do with each other

You for yours - and me for mine
Our reasons crossed paths
And we knew one another
Through the bodies of this time
And co-existed in the space of this place.

A MOTHER'S LOVE

A Mother's love
Is a special love
No one else can understand it
They love us when we're right
And even when we're wrong
If in this life we can return but a part
Of this everlasting love
The joy it brings shown in her heart
And more-so in her deeds
Tells us it was all she needed
Despite our endless fears.

An Invisible Cord 🦋

It is an invisible cord
Our thoughts are connected
I pull - she pulls
I push - she pushes
I try to unwind myself from this
Web of injustice

You will let me be who you taught me to be
But you won't let me be me
I have learned that what society taught you
Is a threat to me
I can only try to not let it imprison me
As it has done to you
How can I make you understand
You being of like mind.

You won't go, and I can't stay
From your limited vision -
The conditioning of your mind
And the love in your heart
You try to give me advice
About a place you've never been
You try to hold me back
In the framework of the familiar
I have got to let it go
The unknown is now my teacher

You have got to put it in perspective
This relationship that we've had
It can grow and even flourish
If we could only find some common ground

The Sword of Truth
Has entered our home
Mother, please let it
Cut the umbilical cord.

MY FIRST LOVE

You come to me at unsuspecting times
And the feeling is Love

I pushed you back
Into the recesses of my mind
And all but forgot
Through the duration of time

You, my first love

You invade my dreams
And destroy my reality
Forcing me to wake
And see what is truly real
Or at least - what is not

I/you love you/me as you/I sit by another

There is no jealousy
There is no
I want to/must be with you
There is no anger
There is no lust

You come to me at unsuspecting times
And the feeling is just

Love.

26

I HAVE THE POWER

To be my own best friend to me
To determine my own destiny

No longer must I/will I depend
Upon a mate or any outside trend
To give me power, to give me strength
To mold my life, or shape my world

Since I began to dis-cover my-Self
And seek the essence that lies within
I found some peace, some dignity
I no longer accept reality

I'm no longer swayed by others advices
I'm no longer paying the guilt-ridden prices
In raising my children or quitting my job
I now realize, it's my hand on the knob

In getting divorced or changing careers
I'm moving my life beyond my own fears
I'm opening doors by instinct alone
Asking others I cannot condone

Although I know not what's on the other side,
My decisions are mine, I make them with pride
I rely on my Self and my God-given strength
My faith will sustain me until I am quenched

(Cont'd.)

I've practiced and preached
And I've strived for and reached
And I've seen for myself
What no others can teach

I'm endowed with the gifts
Of thought and free will
To heal my own life
Or choose to be ill

I'm learning, I'm growing
I'm beginning to flower
I now realize
I have the Power.

This is one of my favorite poems, and many people have come to me and said "I have to have a copy of that poem. I'm going to read it every day." I think this piece is so popular because it can be related to by so many different people. One man who had a history of substance abuse swore that if he could read this poem every day, it would keep him on track. It's amazing to see people become so empowered. I love it. As for me, this poem says it all. In one of my most trying times I dug down into my soul and said "No, I won't succumb. I have the Power."

DON'T STOP

Look for Change in Every Minute
Push yourself to your natural limit

Struggle and Strive
To Top your Tree
And Stand up Tall
So the World can See

Tell them as you're Standing There
That it wasn't Easy or Without a Care

Tell them Now
As you look Back
That it would've been Easier
Had there been no trap

Look Within you'll tell them then
And Take Advice to Lessen the Price

As the fuzzy little worm
Enters his Cocoon
Unaware of the coming
Drastic change - after many moon

So must we - through faith and love
Follow the Same Path

Dig deep inside the Self you've Made
Till you find the Core
And when you think that you have found it
Don't stop till You are Sure.

Call me this
or call me that
I don't care
'cause I am neither

Names point only
to the Presence
Names can never
be the Essence.

In a dimly-lit room
Your fingers touched mine

I promptly lost
All track of
Place
and
Time.

BLACK ANYWAY

Light-skinned, Red-Bone
Oh, and let's not forget
Light, Bright, Damn-Near-White

Those names made me Blacker than any of my friends.
I Became the image of Black

The black leather coat, the applejack hat,
The Kool cigarette hanging from my fingertips
And let's not forget -
The biggest Afro in the hood

I wanted to be Black
I Needed to be accepted
I would have/and did
forfeit my intelligence
In order to be perceived
as what I thought
was Black.

I spoke the downest, hippest,
Blackest English
In order to be perceived as Black
By my own people

Well, here I stand, Tired, Used and Abused
By my own doing as I attempted to escape
From the torment of the illusions/realities
That I created.

(Cont'd.)

I will bend over backwards no more
To be that which I think You need me to be
In order for you to be comfortable, and
Then I can be comfortable.

I don't need to be accepted any more
I don't need to make a point - to me or to you
I make clear conscious choices now.
I no longer re-act out of a need to be
What I perceive as Black

I'm strong, I'm intelligent, I'm good-lookin'
I'm well-spoken, I'm light-skinned
And Guess What -
I'm Black anyway.

Though the Times of Your Life
Contain Struggle and Strife
And You're No Longer Certain
Which Direction is Right

As it Turns and it Bends
With the Times and the Trends
One Path is for Sure
Keep Your Mind on the Lord.

HOW COULD I HAVE KNOWN

What make you think
You can come into my home
Bring all of your belongings
And get on my telephone

You invaded my body
Like an uninvited fix
I want you out of my mind
I want to rid you from my veins

How could I have known
You would reach into my soul
How could I have known
You would make yourself at home.

DON'T CRY FOR ME 🦋

Don't cry for me
As I am gone
Don't lay awake
In the early dawn

With thoughts of grief
Or pity felt
About my life
Or ailing health

I've not gone far
Although from sight
I'm just beyond
Like the day from night

I'm with you still
In the strongest way
I feel your will
All through the day

The bond we shared
And the ways we cared
Are symbols of
Undying love

Be strong in life
And do not fold
Don't let it be said
You just got old

And when you think
You can't go on
That life has made you
Tattered and torn

That's the time
To think of me
That's the time
I'll set you free

(Cont'd.)

You'll feel me with you
You'll know that I'm fine
It'll give you the strength
To keep towing the line

I'm alive and well
On a different plane
I'm alive and you know it
So just stay sane

Don't be consumed
With grief and fear
Of how I died
Or had you been near

The journey we shared
In the physical place
Has blossomed for me
To the cosmic space

I'm sending this message
Because you're in shock
I don't want you to sit
In that chair and just rock

Pick up those pieces
And see which ones fit
Dust yourself off
Take it bit by bit

We came to a fork
In the road that we travelled
No reason to stop
Or become unravelled

Stand on your own
It's a task you must do
And know that I
Will Always Love You.

EYES THAT ARE LOCKED

Although I know it seems unreal
The Power of Your Gaze
Touches somewhere Deep in Me
And We become Engaged

I'm Guided through a Timeless Warp
Wherever you may Lead
Longing for your Passions
And sometimes for your Seed

It's getting hard to Resist
That very first Kiss
'cause I'm Needing you more
Than I care to Admit

I feel like a Pawn
On a giant Chess Board
Like a Grain of Sand
On an Ocean Floor

It's Futile to Fight
With all of my Might

For through Eyes that are Locked
And Time that has Stopped
We Journey through Space
In a Cosmic Embrace

Merging from Two to One.

IN THE HEAT OF ANGER

Sometimes in the Heat of Anger
Some Things Get Said
That Aren't Really Meant

Feelings Get Hurt
Via Crushed Expectations
People Get Lost
In Seas of Emotions
Each Reacting to the Other's Insults

But Somewhere - In the Eye of the Hurricane
I Want to Grab You - and Hold You
I Want us to Fuse Together
Totally Understand Each Other
And All That Surrounds Us

I Want Us To Find Each Other
In That Same Sea
And Become Cleansed by Waves of Love
And Washed Ashore to Begin Anew

Sometimes in the Heat of Anger
Some Things Get Said
That Aren't Really Meant.

I HAD LOVED

I had loved
And I had lost
And I thought
That I was through

I gave up on
That special someone
I gave up on
Looking for you

When you came I did not see
Who you really were to me
I had retreated into my shell
I was content - It was complete

But you knocked so long
And you knocked so hard
On the door that
Hid my heart

I had to crack it
Just to peek
I would have been
Oh, so discreet

But I saw you
And you saw me
I slammed the door
And turned the key

I tried to run
But turned to look
You were there
Inside my heart.

TO MY MOM WITH LOVE

Just a note from me to say
In my thoughts you are today
But more importantly it's true
The times are often I think of you

For all my life you've given me
Support and love for all to see
And though at times it may not show
I hope my love - you'll all ways know.

Thank You For Loving Me
In a Space Where there is No Place
Nor Time

Thank You For Loving Me
In a Way that Knows No Words
Nor Rhyme

Thank You For Loving Me
Without End

Thank You For Being
My Friend.

In the ocean of life
we tread and we played
In another moment we
found ourselves
standing waist deep
in clear silk water
near a secluded shore
face to face
wrapped in a tender embrace
unable to let go
fully clothed
basking in our own nakedness
and the warm sun
we held each other
not daring to move a muscle.

To My Husband, With Love
Respect and Admiration

Walking Together on the Path of Life
Is What We've Chosen To Do
It Works So Well I Often Wonder
Did We Choose It or Was It Fate
I Was Happy Before
But I'm Happier Now
I Hope That Will Always Remain
'Cause We Work Together,
We Love Together
You're My Partner, My Lover, My Friend.

Tain't no time for cryin'
'bout where we been
and who we ain't

Tain't no time
for self indulgence
'bout who done what
and got away

Now's the time
to jump for joy
Teaching every
girl and boy

Drop the chains that
wrap your mind
Do it now
and you will find

That the chains
that used to bind us
Need only serve
to remind us

We're not bound
by physical means
We have become
Kings and Queens.

I LOVE YOU . . . STILL

There were moments we shared
That I'll never forget
When our bodies united
. . . And only eyes met

There were times when we two
Were one and the same
And I would have answered
. . . To even your name

There were moments we shared
That I'll never forget
When our souls united
And I loved you . . . Yet

Somehow this happened
In the face of the sea
As I tried to love you
. . . Unconditionally

Where there's pain, there's growth
Of this I'm sure
But still when this happened
. . . I ran for the door

As I gave you my back
And I tried to refrain
I was gently reminded
Where there's growth, there's pain

(Cont'd.)

46

As I struggled and fought
Using all of my will
The message went through me
I love you . . . still

In the face of the battle
Do I turn and I run
Is that how to succeed
Is that how it's won?

I tossed and I turned
And I wrestled all night
Until I soon realized
It's my mind that I fight

The lesson was mine
To avoid or to learn
I had to go through it
The bruises I've earned

I now know the answer
But, is it too late
Can I pick up the pieces
Have I sealed my own fate?

Whatever your answer
However you feel
I respect your decision
I know you'll be real.

Here's To You
In Your Moment of Glory
What A Wonderful Time
What a Beautiful Story

Here's To Your Dream
As It Finally Comes True
Here's To The Love
Shared By Just You

Here's To Achievement
Of All Of Your Goals
Here's To The Union
Of Two Beautiful Souls

*You looked at me and
Stopped Time*

Blew my Mind

*Sent Pins and Needles
Up and Down my Spine*

*Rocked my Soul
Don't you Be so Bold*

*Gave me Chills and Thrills
and Stood my Hair on End*

*Baby, Please -
Won't cha Look at Me Again.*

STRAIGHT TO THE TOP

Well I'd like to stop
And I'd like to chat
And I'd like to give you
Tit for Tat

But I don't even really
Have time for that
Because Straight to the Top
Is where I'm Headed

You see Right at the Top
Is Where you'll find me

I don't have Time
To Stop and Stare
And I don't have Time
To Primp with Hair

You see My Direction
Is oh, so Clear
I've got to keep on Movin'
No time for Fear

I've gotta keep Goin'
At a Steady Pace
I can't go too Fast
Because 'Haste makes Waste'

I've gotta get up Early
And go to bed late
Because Sac-ri-fice
Is Now Part of my Fate

(Cont'd.)

You see Determination
Is my Best Friend
It takes Perseverance
Right to the End

It gets kinda Rough
But I can't Pause
I've gotta ride this wave, Brother
I've Got a Cause

This is the Wave that
Sets Me Free
You see, My Success

Is Waiting For Me.

AIR

Thank you God
For blessing me
With Life's most precious
Necessity

For as You've given
Air to breathe
I know You'll satisfy
My needs

You cannot phone
Nor can You write
But the message You send
Is clear tonight

What need I
Of doubt or fear
Of how to live
Without a care

For as You've given
Air to breathe
What more could I
A human, need

You've given me strength
And tools to build
A life of love
That's beauty filled

(cont'd.)

What more could I
Possibly need
To prove to me
I am Your seed

There is no way
I can not know
No way to say
It does not show

For, God, I feel You
In my lungs
I know from Your loin
I have sprung

And in my daily
Mundane chores
I know I am
A child of Yours

And as I open
Each new door
I know that I'm
Provided for

For, God, my Father
You've given me
Life's most Basic
Necessity.

RECEIVING MORE

What idea
Has died in me
And brought about
This poverty

And what is the thought
Remaining in tact
That brings about
This life of lack

When something dies
It also gives
The message is
That something lives

There is no one
Without the other
There is no child
Lest there be a mother

If you see
And if you hear
You can learn
The thoughts held dear

(Cont'd.)

For thoughts held deep
Within your mind
They come about
With passing time

When will the thought
Of poverty die
And shine the light
Upon the lie

Receiving more
Lives in the death
Of wanting more
Yet accepting less.

Seminars Available:

Future by Design or Default

Begin to Win – Now

*Resolving Conflict through Understanding and
Anger Management*

Strategies for Success — the Working Woman's Seminar

*Achieving Effective & Professional Customer Service and
Telephone Skills
Get that Job! Resumés — to Interviews — to Job Offers!*

For More Information Please Contact:

*McRae Enterprises
P. O. Box 230174
Hollis Station, NY 11423
(212) 769-7918
(888) 572-2146
ReneeMcRae@usa.com*